DISCIPLESHIP

Engage in the Great Commission
and Create a Lasting Impact

RIVER LYNN

Brently Pennington

**Victory Vision Publishing & Consulting, LLC
PO Box 1144
Amarillo, TX 79105**

Copyright © 2021
by Brently Pennington

All rights reserved, including the right to reproduce this book or portions thereof in any form whatsoever. No part of this book may be reproduced, stored in a retrieval system, or transmitted by any means without the author's written permission. For information, address Victory Vision Publishing & Consulting, LLC at the above address.

Scriptures referred to in this book are taken from the most up to date translations of the Holy Bible published by Zondervan Publishing House and provided online by Biblegateway.com.

First paperback edition January 2021

Manufactured in the United States of America

ISBN: 9798581955536

DEDICATION

To Dad and Mom
The greatest disciple-makers I know.
Thank you for discipling me.

CONTENTS

	Acknowledgments	i
	Endorsement	iii
	Preface	iv
1	My Story	1
2	Who Can Disciple?	9
3	Why Discipleship?	15
4	Jesus, The Ultimate Example of Discipleship	23
5	Other Examples of Discipleship in Scripture	29
6	Discipleship in Parenting	35
7	The Key Role of Mentorship	39
8	Methods for Discipleship	43
9	Don't Quit!	55
10	Just Start!	63
	Bibliography	66
	About the Author	67

ACKNOWLEDGMENTS

I want to thank my family and friends who have supported me in this endeavor. I want to thank Landry Lockett and Steve Allen for encouraging me to write my first book and for supporting me during the process. I want to thank Olivia and Joy for editing my book and significantly improving it! I want to thank Julie Ballard and Victory Vision Publishing for making this possible. I want to thank all those who contributed testimonies. All of your stories are powerful examples of the beauty of discipleship. Thank you for discipling others and making a lasting impact. I am honored to know you. I want to thank my parents, who supported me through this process and who first discipled me. They are my heroes and my example of what it means to disciple others. I want to thank Jesus for loving me, saving me, and for giving me purpose. He is the reason for this book.

ENDORSEMENT

Paul exhorts his spiritual son Philemon to share his faith at all times. One of the serendipities of sharing your faith is that you will be encouraged in the Lord. This book on discipleship by River Lynn will be a powerful tool in your hands. River is the real deal! She has been in the hardest and darkest places on the earth, sharing her faith. She loves the lost and is a stellar example of one who is light and salt to all those around them. You will be blessed to read this book and apply it to your life!

Steve Allen
Allen Leadership Coaching
Author of And He Ran for 40 Days

PREFACE

"And what you have heard from me in the presence of many witnesses entrust to faithful men, who will be able to teach others also."

2 Timothy 2:2 ESV

This verse has changed my life. It has dictated how I live and has given me a perspective on how to impact and reach people. I still remember looking at this verse with my uncle, in beautiful Colorado, in my grandparents' home during my college years.

We were sitting at the kitchen table with a gorgeous mountain view discussing life and the ways of God. My uncle opened the Bible, and he took me to this verse, saying, "This is what you are called to do. It is worth giving your life for."

Looking back, that was a moment that changed my life forever. I have been marked by many men and women who have impacted me through practicing this verse. They embodied what Paul did for Timothy by entrusting the teachings of Jesus to me. Their investment has empowered me to teach others also.

The purpose of this book is to empower you to go and make disciples because Jesus is worth it.

As you read the words in this book, my prayer for you is that you would be filled with courage to disciple, envisioned as to how you can make a lasting impact, and inspired to change the world. May you continue to grow in the knowledge of Jesus and go and make disciples.

Emem- Young professional

In college, I was a part of a Bible study group. After graduation, I transitioned to discipling others, which has led to so much spiritual growth, and my faith seems unshakable. Today, I have the opportunity to disciple three other girls and pour into them, and I know the cycle will not end with them. There's power in having someone study the Word with you and walk with you in your faith.

CHAPTER ONE
MY STORY

My own personal journey of discipling others started when I was in college, but my discipleship journey actually began in childhood. I had many men and women, including my parents pouring into my life, just as Timothy's mother, grandmother, and Paul did for Timothy. They invested in me as fathers and mothers in the faith. They encouraged me to pursue the Lord first and foremost, and they taught me to seek His ways by following the example of Jesus. I grew up memorizing scripture and hearing the Gospel. I witnessed examples of men and women who had given their lives for the sake of Jesus. I am forever grateful for their impact and influence on my life.

When I was eighteen years old, I was significantly impacted by a Bible study that I had done during the summer before college. It was a study on the Song of Solomon focusing on Jesus' love for us. This study greatly impacted me and gave me more confidence in Jesus' love for me.

I didn't realize it then, but that study prepared me for what the Lord had for me that fall. I see now how He was strengthening my faith and giving me courage through obtaining a deeper understanding of the depths of God's love for me. A few weeks later, I started classes at my university. I moved into my college dorm and met my roommate, who was also an incoming freshman. As I got to know her, I learned that she believed in Jesus, but she didn't know much about who He was. As our friendship grew, she expressed interest in learning more about Jesus, and my journey of discipling others began.

I was home for the weekend, and I was telling my parents about the situation. My dad turned to me and asked me a question that changed my life. He said, "Why can't you disciple her? Why not you?" This question hit me to the core, and immediately I felt intimidated and afraid. I had never taught someone the Bible intentionally and consistently like this before. I felt deeply inadequate, insecure, and unqualified at that moment. I instantly started making excuses,

"I couldn't be the one to disciple her. I'm not qualified. I'm only eighteen. I don't know how to teach the Bible."

My dad looked at me and said, "You can do it, and you must do it."

"But how?" I asked.

He looked at me and smiled and said, "Just take what you've been learning in the Bible and share it with your roommate."

I had no excuses left at that moment, and I knew I had to do it. Because if I didn't do it, who would? She was my roommate, and I believed God had brought her into my life for a purpose. She wanted to know more about Jesus, and I knew Him. How could I keep the good news about Him inside and keep her from learning about how wonderful He is and starting a relationship with Him?

I now was afforded an opportunity to be obedient to Jesus and trust Him to help me do what He was calling me to do. So, I said yes. I stepped out on the waters, insecure and afraid but willing. I learned through this step that this is what Jesus is after. A willing heart.

Looking back, I had no idea how impactful this yes would be and how it would start the trajectory for the rest of my life. Within the next few days, I asked my roommate if she would want to study the Bible with me, and she said yes. What I thought would be a 1-1 Bible study with my roommate quickly turned into a Bible study with five girls joining. We met once a week in my tiny little dorm room that had no air conditioning. It was hot and crowded and wonderful all at the same time! We would sit on the floor, and to be honest, I didn't know what I was doing. I just knew I had to teach them the Bible.

I knew I had to make disciples, and I knew that meant teaching people to obey Jesus' commands. So, we opened up the Word of God together, and I used some sermon notes I found online to help me start discussions. (If you need help starting, there are many resources available today that can help you lead a Bible study. I will share some tips on how to conduct one in Chapter 8 on the "Methods of Discipleship.")

When I started a Bible study with five girls the first semester of my freshman year, I quickly realized the joy found in declaring scripture and seeing people come alive and be transformed by the Word of God. It is not by your own weak words, but by His Word that transformation happens! That Bible study group continued through all eight semesters of my college experience. Every semester, we would study a different book in the Bible, and each semester the study was unique. Other girls would come and go, and the number of people attending fluctuated, but we kept going all the way through my college years. Thankfully, we were also able to change locations to the local chapel on our campus, and it had air conditioning! I learned so much through this journey of discipling others.

As I began to share the Word of God with these girls, I started to grow in my knowledge of the Bible, and I began to hunger for more understanding. I learned something significant in that season, and it's changed my entire life. I learned not to wait until you feel ready to disciple others. Instead, just start somewhere, and you will learn along the way!

You don't have to wait for someone to recognize you as a leader and tell you that now you're ready to disciple others. You don't have to wait until you have a Ph.D. in theology. You can do it right now with what is in your hands. If you are a disciple of Jesus, you can disciple others. Jesus is the one who qualifies you, and as long as you stay humble and open to hearing His voice, He will guide and lead you. There will be challenges along the way. You will make mistakes. But do not let fear and intimidation keep you from obeying Jesus' command in the Great Commission to make disciples.

As college continued, I started thinking about graduation and how I wanted to see this discipleship group continue even after I left. I wanted to leave a lasting legacy of people who would continue to disciple others. I met several girls going into my senior year who I felt God was highlighting for me to disciple. I began meeting with them weekly to teach them the Word and encourage them to make disciples. Over time, they began leading their own Bible studies. As I graduated from college and moved away, the discipleship continued through several of these women.

As I write this book, I received a message from a girl that I'm currently discipling. She is a freshman at my alumni university, and she started a Bible study with other freshmen on our campus. She even had one of her meetings in the same chapel I used while I was in college. Five years later, students are still being discipled. When you intentionally commit to discipling others, it can make a lasting impact. You may never know how great an impact you have made through simple obedience on this side of eternity. People are being impacted by the truth of the Gospel shared by Jesus' disciples every day. When you impact even just one life, it matters to God. That life can impact more lives than you could ever reach. Discipleship has the ability to change the world.

After leaving college, I continued to look for different opportunities to disciple others. Today, much of my discipleship takes place via long-distance phone calls. Several of the girls I disciple live in various locations globally, so we have weekly phone calls.

I also practice discipleship with my younger siblings, who are fourteen and seventeen years old. I had young adults pour into my life when I was a teenager, and I want my siblings to have the same opportunity. I have a passion for discipleship as I have seen how effective it can be. I have a passion for seeing people transformed by the Word of God, and I have a desire to see this become the passion of the body of Christ all across the earth.

I'm encouraged to share that several of the women I've discipled are now making disciples themselves. They are making a lasting impact through sharing the Gospel and teaching people God's Word. If I can do it as an 18-year-old and now as a 27-year-old, you can too! Jesus is worth it!

DISCIPLESHIP

Emma – College Student

My mentor poured into me and discipled me. She taught me and continues to teach me about the Word and how sweet our God is. She has been fundamental in helping me understand my role in sharing the name of Jesus. As I entered college, I stumbled upon a group of women entering school at the same time as I was. They all had a desire to study the Bible together and enter college with eyes on the Lord. God led me to volunteer to guide them in a discipleship group before realizing what I had agreed to. When I told my mentor, she was so excited and was able to speak life into me despite my fear and self-doubt. I started off terrified, but by returning to the example set before me by my mentor, I began leading a group of phenomenal women. Our study group has grown so much in number and wisdom. The growth that I've seen in these women, individually, is so beautiful and such a testament to what God does when we seek Him in a strong community. As a group, I've seen motivation that keeps us going each week and pure joy in reading the Bible. We have a bond built upon the foundation of Christ, and God has poured out his favor on us. The women I am blessed to be discipling are chasing after the Lord, and I'm so thankful that I get to run alongside them.

CHAPTER TWO
WHO CAN DISCIPLE?

The first experience of discipling my roommate and her friends in college permanently changed my mindset on discipleship. I realized that discipleship is for every believer. Every believer should be discipled and should disciple others. I saw that it wasn't too hard or too complicated, but through the empowerment of the Holy Spirit, it is possible! My excuses based on fears and insecurities were disempowered when I discovered the power that Jesus offers. I am called to be a disciple-maker, and so are you!

Unfortunately, many believers have discounted themselves from discipleship just like I did. Many haven't experienced discipleship in their own lives and thus don't have an understanding of what it is. Others may have been discipled, but fears and insecurities weigh them down and prevent them from engaging in discipling others. There is a great need for discipleship in the earth in this hour, and we, as the Body of Christ, must respond and engage in it for the sake of Jesus and His mission. Discipleship is for everyone. Men and women, young and old, and all believers can (and should!) disciple others.

DISCIPLESHIP

The word disciple in Greek μαθητής (*mathētēs*) generally refers to any "student," "pupil," "apprentice," or "adherent"[1] We, as believers in Jesus, are called to be His disciples. Discipleship, simply put, is teaching and training people to become faithful followers of Jesus. We are teaching people the Bible, and we are training them on how to obey the words of scripture.

We are not raising up disciples for ourselves, but for Jesus. Peter describes this in 1 Peter 5:4 when He refers to Jesus as the chief Shepherd.

"And when the chief Shepherd appears, you will receive the unfading crown of glory."
1 Peter 5:4 ESV

This scripture refers to the return of Christ, our chief Shepherd. When you are discipling, you take upon the role of a shepherd who is shepherding God's people. However, it is essential to remember who the Chief is and who you are leading the sheep to. You are leading them to Jesus. The book of Jeremiah speaks of the reality of discipleship. God declares, *"And I will give you shepherds after my own heart, who will feed you with knowledge and understanding* (Jer 3:15 ESV)." God desires that shepherds would arise who would shepherd His people. We want to be people

---

[1] Understanding the Meaning of the Term "Disciple"

who go after God's own heart and who shepherd others to do the same.

Discipleship is demonstrating through your daily walk what it means to be a follower of Jesus. Discipleship is walking alongside someone and equipping them to fulfill their God-given potential and assignment. The purpose of discipleship is to raise up wholehearted faithful followers of Jesus. Discipleship can occur before someone is saved as a way to lead them to salvation by teaching them the Word of God. Discipleship should also occur after salvation to help the person you are discipling grow in maturity through instruction in God's Word.

We see numerous examples in scripture of people from all different walks of life discipling others. We see the example of the twelve men who Jesus personally selected to disciple. We witness Paul's discipleship of Timothy and Titus. We examine the story of Mary of Bethany sitting at the feet of Jesus in Luke 10:38-42, which was a posture that a disciple of a rabbi would take. At that time, it was unprecedented for a woman to be discipled by a rabbi, yet Jesus welcomed her to listen and learn from Him.

In Acts 18:24-28, we see Priscilla and Aquilla's story, a married couple discipling a Jew named Apollos, who was competent in the scriptures but needed further instructions on the teachings of Jesus. This is both an example of a woman discipling and an example of a husband and wife discipling someone together. Deborah was a woman who discipled the nation of Israel. Her story is found in Judges 4 and 5.

We see Timothy's example as a young person being exhorted to disciple other people in 2 Timothy 2:2. In the same verse, we witness Paul as an older man discipling Timothy. In Titus 2:3-5, Paul instructs older women to teach younger women. The Bible clearly demonstrates that both men and women of all ages and levels of position and power are able, and more importantly, called to disciple.

A disciple-maker is not a personality type. You don't have to be the most incredible speaker. You don't have to be an extrovert. You don't have to be social or outgoing. Anyone can disciple, and all believers must disciple because we want to see the Great Commission fulfilled. Jesus is worth it. The reason we disciple is ultimately for Jesus' glory. He is our reason, and He is our purpose. Discipleship is a privilege and should be an integral part of the life of every follower of Jesus.

DISCIPLESHIP

Priscilla- College Student

In January 2018, during my freshman year of college, the Lord challenged me to start discipling others, and then He highlighted my friend Michelle. I found out that she had been praying and asking God for someone to disciple her. We began this journey of discipleship together weekly. After eight months, she moved to Korea, and she began discipling people in a very similar way. I learned through this experience that discipleship multiplies. You may not know how many people are affected by your "yes" to discipleship. Your reach may even be extended unto the nations! I have now discipled 16 people to date, both individually and through group discipleship. God has taught me that discipleship involves dependence on Him. I am passionate about discipleship because not only am I able to help others grow in their walk with Jesus, but I have found that I also grow as I disciple others. You don't have to have all the answers because no one does. We have the source, the Holy Spirit in us, who knows all the answers. Anyone can disciple if they do it in a spirit of humility and dependence on Jesus. It is possible!

DISCIPLESHIP

CHAPTER THREE
WHY DISCIPLESHIP?

Discipleship matters to God because people matter to God. God desires that *"none would perish, but all would come to repentance (2 Pet 3:9)."* We disciple others because Jesus commanded us to do it.

The Great Commission is our God-given assignment. It is what Jesus commanded us to do before He ascended into heaven. Matthew 28:18-20 says, *"And Jesus came and said to them, 'All authority in heaven and on earth has been given to me. Go therefore and make disciples of all nations, baptizing them in the name of the Father and of the Son and of the Holy Spirit, teaching them to observe all that I have commanded you. And behold, I am with you always, to the end of the age.'"*

Jesus calls us to go and make disciples of all nations. We are called to baptize them in the name of the Father, Son, and Holy Spirit and teach them to obey all that he has commanded us. His promise in this is that He will never leave us or forsake us. He is always with you! That is the greatest comfort on this journey of discipleship. The God above all things, the Creator of the heavens and the earth, the First and the Last, the great I Am is with *you*. He will never leave you, and He will empower you to do what He has called you to do.

In 2 Timothy 2:2, Paul gives a concise and clear description of discipleship. In his letter to Timothy, Paul speaks as a father to his spiritual son, and he encourages him to take what he learned from him and entrust it to faithful men who will be able to teach others. This is one of the clearest pictures of discipleship. It is taking the truths of the Word of God and entrusting it to others, who in turn are faithful to entrust it to others and so on.

This is what we are called to do and what it looks like to walk as a disciple-maker. We are to live like Jesus, who was the greatest disciple-maker of all. Paul tells Timothy the teachings of Jesus as an *apostolic* witness, an intimate retelling, in the presence of many witnesses. Many believe this might be a reference to Timothy's ordination service found in 1 Timothy 6:12. Paul instructs Timothy to entrust those teachings to faithful men who will be able to teach others also. He uses the word "faithful" to describe the type of person he is encouraging Timothy to invest in. He instructs Timothy to entrust these teachings to faithful men who will be faithful to continue to share it with others.

DISCIPLESHIP

And what you have heard from me in the presence of many witnesses entrust to faithful men, who will be able to teach others also.

2 Timothy 2:2 (ESV)

Here, the word "men" is the Greek word *"anthropoi,"* which can refer to both men and women, depending on the context[2]. The key idea in this verse is multiplication, one person passing on the teachings of Jesus to others, and so on. We see four generations of discipleship: Jesus to Paul, Paul to Timothy, Timothy to faithful men, and faithful men to others[3]. This verse clearly illustrates that multiplication is at the heart of discipleship. I like to refer to it as the 222-discipleship verse to make it easy to remember. If you impact one person and if that person impacts another person, who in turn impacts another person and so on, multitudes can be transformed.

In his speech at the University of Texas in 2014, Admiral William McRaven exhorted the graduating class to be world changers. "Tonight, there are almost 8,000 students graduating from UT. That great paragon of analytical rigor, ask.com, says that the average American will meet 10,000 people in their lifetime. That's a lot of folks. But, if every one of you changed the lives of just ten people — and

---

[2] From the Footnote on Bible Gateway 2 Timothy 2:2
[3] 5 Steps for Disciple Multiplication

each one of those folks changed the lives of another ten people — just ten — then in five generations — 125 years — the class of 2014 will have changed the lives of Eight hundred million people. Eight hundred million people — think of it — over twice the population of the United States. Go one more generation, and you can change the entire population of the world — eight billion people."[4]

McRaven's speech describes the power of discipleship by impacting the lives of as many people as possible through the proclamation of the Gospel message. This our aim, and through the method of discipleship such as that seen in the life of Jesus, Paul, and many others in scripture, we have the ability to have a global impact. This simple example shows the power and potential of discipleship. Imagine if every believer in the world shared their faith with, and faithfully discipled, at least ten other people in their lifetime; we could see the world as a whole evangelized!

So why do we disciple? Because Jesus told us to do it, and as His followers, we must obey Him. The fact that discipleship was the last command before He ascended into heaven highlights its importance. The last words of an individual are significant. Jesus' final words to His disciples show that we must take

---
[4] Adm. McRaven Urges Graduates to Find Courage to Change the World.

discipleship seriously. Unfortunately, the enemy has tried to deceive the church over the years by making many believe that discipleship is too challenging, too difficult, and only for pastors or people in ministry. The devil hates discipleship, and he will combat it in any way that he can. His main tactics are fear and intimidation. Don't believe the lie that you aren't good enough to disciple others, but instead silence this lie by standing on truth in scripture that every believer is called to disciple; it is an integral part of the Christian life and something that God empowers us to do through the Holy Spirit.

Reflection Questions:

What has your discipleship journey looked like to date? Have you ever been discipled by others before, or do you have experience discipling others?

After reading this chapter, do you believe that discipleship is a central part of our call as followers of Jesus?

Is there anything blocking you from engaging with discipleship? Fear, age, experience?

DISCIPLESHIP

Jake - College Student

One summer, while I was in college, I was working at Walmart. I met a fellow co-worker named Josh. He said that he saw that my lifestyle was different than the other co-workers. I told him that I was a Christian, and Jesus was the reason I lived differently. He was inquisitive, and he began to ask me questions. I started sharing with him about Jesus. I encouraged him to read the Bible and start going to church to gain community. Later that fall, while I was back at university, my dad met a Walmart employee who began to share his testimony. He shared how he had been working there and how he'd felt really discouraged about how his life was going. Then he met a guy who was different, and he wanted what he had. He said that he began to read the Bible and started going to church. "Now, I am a leader in the youth group at my church, and I take kids on mission trips. My life is completely changed!" My dad asked him the name of the guy who had shared with him about Jesus only to discover that it was me, his son, who had discipled this man. Jesus has the power to transform lives, and He can use your life as a witness to disciple others.

DISCIPLESHIP

CHAPTER FOUR
JESUS, THE ULTIMATE
EXAMPLE OF DISCIPLESHIP

When we start to look at discipleship and begin thinking about how we can practice it in our lives, we can look to Jesus as the ultimate example and teacher. We see that He changed the world by discipling a small group of individuals. They changed the world, not because they were the smartest or the brightest, but because they were entrusted with the message of the Gospel, and they were obedient in sharing it boldly with those God entrusted to them.

Jesus spoke to the multitudes, but he focused both on the individuals and smaller groups. He knew the impact that can happen even with one individual or small groups of people. A life laid down in obedience to the Father, engaging in authentic discipleship is very powerful, even if it's just for one other person.

Jesus knew the power of discipleship, and He called the least likely individuals to be a part of His ministry. He chose tax collectors, fishermen, and zealots. He chose people that many in society would overlook. He allowed a woman, Mary of Bethany, to sit at his feet and be discipled by Him. Jesus chose ordinary people, many of whom were on the fringes of society, to follow Him. Through their obedience and pursuit of Him, *they* changed the world.

When you ask the question, "Who do I disciple? What does it look like?" you should look to Jesus' example.

1. **Prayer**

    He began His journey of discipleship in prayer, communicating with the Father. We should follow the example that He set in Luke 6:12-16. We want to disciple people that God is highlighting for us to disciple. We want to hear God's voice and be obedient to who He's calling us to invest in. Ask God for wisdom to lead and guide you to the person or persons he asks you to disciple.

2. **Invitation**

    Following prayer, Jesus called His disciples to follow him. He didn't wait for people to come to Him and ask Him if he could disciple them. He went to them and gave them the invitation to follow Him. The same can be said for us. It is less likely for someone to come to you and ask you to disciple them. It happens sometimes, but it's more of a rarity than the norm. When asking someone to be discipled by you, it is important that you are clear of your intentions and give them the opportunity to respond to your invitation. This will help you to call out those people who are serious about being discipled. It is also important to clarify that you are ultimately leading them to better follow in *Christ's* footsteps and *not* your own.

3. **Teaching**

   Jesus regularly took the time to teach both His disciples and His wider followers. He was known as a rabbi, which means teacher.[5] He used parables to convey the truths of the Kingdom. He also boldly proclaimed the Gospel and instructed them to follow His ways and teach others also. With this in mind, it is essential to make sure Jesus' example and teaching, as found in God's Word, is central to your discipleship. You want to be teaching others to follow God's Word and Jesus' example, *not your own*.

4. **Living Example**

   Jesus did life with His disciples. He ate with them, traveled with them, and even went to celebrations with them, such as the wedding at Cana recorded in John 2. They were not just His disciples but also His friends and His

---

[5] Merriam Webster Dictionary

community. He lived His life amongst them in a way that they could learn from His example. He also walked in a spirit of humility as described in Philippians 2:5-11. He operated in the fruits of the Spirit as detailed in Galatians 5:22-23. As you disciple someone, often, your actions will speak louder than your words. Paul states, *"Be imitators of me, as I am of Christ* (1 Cor 11:1 ESV)." As you walk in obedience to the Father, and you focus your life on becoming more like Jesus, you can just as confidently say, "Imitate me as I imitate Christ!"

5. **Sending**

Jesus sent out those who He discipled to go and make disciples. In Luke 10:1-24, He sent out the seventy-two in twos to make disciples. In Matthew 28:18-20, Jesus gave the Great Commission and commissioned His followers to make disciples. As you disciple people, continually encourage them to look for opportunities where they can share what they are learning in order to disciple others. Empower them to do what you are doing.

Reflection Question:

Who is the Lord inviting you to disciple?

Rebecca – Mom

I was once introduced to a girl who had endured some pretty tough circumstances and desperately needed a friend. I soon realized what she really needed was a friendship with Jesus, so I asked if we could meet consistently and study the Bible. She agreed, and discipleship began. The more we met, it was clear that her beautiful life was suffering from past wounds and the ill effects of impurity. She struggled for security and was guarded. Months and months went by, and I saw very little outward change. I was discouraged, but because I felt strongly from God to keep pursuing her, we continued to meet. Over time, however, she began to tenderize under the power of the Word. As we read out loud, her eyes would fill with tears. One day, we read and talked about how we are His sheep who know His voice. She began to listen and, wow, did He begin to speak! She started showing up to our meetings, bursting with testimonies. She would tell me how the Holy Spirit had convicted her of this and that, how she began reading the Bible consistently in her own spare time, how she would talk to Him regularly, even how she had initiated with a co-worker to begin meeting up to read the Bible just as we had. Today, she is a different person! The challenging circumstances of her life have not seen much change, but she is equipped. She has become a friend of Jesus. She knows His voice and loves His Truth.

CHAPTER FIVE
OTHER EXAMPLES OF
DISCIPLESHIP IN SCRIPTURE

Alongside Jesus' example of discipleship, we see many other examples in scripture of people discipling others. One of them is Paul the Apostle. As we saw in 2 Timothy 2:2, Paul discipled Timothy, Titus, and many others. He was an effective and fruitful disciple-maker. He was one who boldly preached the Gospel and served as a living example to others, especially pouring into younger men like Timothy and Titus.

Timothy met Paul when he was still a teenager, and he went on to become an essential church planter with Paul. In Acts 16:1-17:14, we see that Timothy assisted Paul in establishing churches at Philippi, Thessalonica, and Berea. Timothy's life was marked with a passion for Jesus. Under his mother, grandmother, and Paul's training, he went from an ordinary teenager to a prolific leader in the early church. Timothy gave his life for the advancement of the Gospel.

Titus was another young man whom Paul discipled. Titus was a Greek unbeliever who heard Paul's proclamation of the Gospel and responded.

Paul recalls his experience with Titus in Galatians 2:1-4. Scripture informs us in Titus 1:4-5 that Paul and Titus went to Crete to proclaim the Gospel there, but Paul left him there to continue traveling. Paul trusted Titus to be a faithful witness of Christ, even in his absence[6].

The books of 1st and 2nd Timothy and Titus are books where Paul speaks directly to his disciples. These letters are examples of how he addressed them and interacted with them. He addresses them as a father addresses his sons. He was deeply committed to their lives and deeply committed to their success. He stewarded his relationship with them in a way that they were empowered to continue preaching and proclaiming the Gospel even after he left.

Paul understood that true, authentic discipleship creates a legacy. When you are gone, you want the people behind you to be able to continue sharing the truths of the Gospel just as effectively as you. Like Paul, when you die, you want to leave behind a legacy of people who are making disciples. As a worldwide church, we want to see the Great Commission fulfilled, which happens through discipleship.

Another example of discipleship is found in the story of Elijah and Elisha. The account of their

---

[6] Who Were Timothy And Titus?

meeting is found in 1 Kings 19:19-21. In this story, we see Elijah inviting Elisha into a discipleship relationship. He threw his cloak over Elisha, and Elisha accepted the invitation to follow Elijah. Then in 2 Kings 2:1-18, we see the story of Elijah being taken up into heaven in a whirlwind. Before Elijah was taken up into heaven, he asked Elisha what he could do for him before he was taken away. Elisha asked for a double portion of Elijah's spirit to rest upon him. Elisha's tenacity and passion for more of God is an incredible example of the heart posture we should embody when we engage in discipleship. As disciple-makers, we should ask the Lord to highlight the people who have Elisha's passion for pursuing God and desiring more. And as disciples, we should ask for tenacity and passion like Elisha.

A final example I'll share is the discipleship relationship between Moses and Joshua. In Exodus 33:11, we see how Moses would speak face to face with the Lord inside the Tent of Meeting. After he was finished, he would return to the camp, but Joshua would not depart from the Tabernacle. Moses' relationship with the Lord provoked Joshua to desire more in his own walk with the Lord. This relationship is a beautiful example of how we, as disciple-makers, can inspire and motivate others to pursue the Lord for themselves after witnessing our walk with the Lord. Moses led the people of Israel

DISCIPLESHIP

with Joshua learning from his example. When Moses' time of leading the people ended, Joshua was equipped to lead the people into the promised land. His season of training under Moses' leadership taught him the importance of seeking the face of God for himself, and he was then able to lead his people into the promised land while seeking the Lord for wisdom and guidance as a leader.

DISCIPLESHIP

Reflection Questions:

Which example of discipleship, either from above or in scripture, stands out to you the most? What can you learn from their example?

Choose a few other examples of discipleship in scripture to study and ask the same question: What can I learn from their example?

Spend some time in prayer and ask God from these examples, what area(s) He specifically wants you to develop in this season.

Tracy - Mom

My journey of discipleship began in high school when my youth leader began to disciple me. I was so impacted by this season that it set me on a trajectory towards discipling others. When I became a stay at home, homeschooling mom, I chose to use that unique season to disciple younger women. I would invite these women into my life as a mom; cooking, cleaning, teaching school, and changing diapers. They saw the beautiful, messy chaos of my life raising six children. I would listen to their stories, teach them about Jesus, and share my own experiences of walking with Him. I rarely had a moment to really sit down with them for an extended time, so I just invited them into my world and used it as an opportunity to train them to be disciples of Jesus as well as future godly wives and mothers. At the time, it often felt small and insignificant, but years later, their testimonies have encouraged me that I did make a difference even when it felt weak or lacking. Whatever season you are in, ask the Lord to highlight who He is calling you to pour into and see what He can do with your "yes!"

CHAPTER SIX
DISCIPLESHIP IN PARENTING

Parents are called to disciple. Timothy's initial training began at home under the care and teaching of his mother and grandmother. Paul describes the impact that Timothy's grandmother and mother had on their son and grandson.

"I am reminded of your sincere faith, a faith that dwelt first in your grandmother Lois and your mother Eunice and now, I am sure, dwells in you as well."
2 Timothy 1:5 ESV.

We can see that the impact of Timothy's grandmother and mother were instrumental in helping Timothy become the man he was called to be. I firmly believe that parenting is the most significant discipleship opportunity that is available. Children are under the care of their parents for their formative years, and parents have the privilege and responsibility to train them up in the ways of the Lord. Fathers and Mothers have been given a unique opportunity to disciple their children daily, and their influence can have a tremendous impact on their children's journey towards the Lord.

DISCIPLESHIP

Both of my parents were so instrumental in my discipleship journey. Growing up, my mother not only discipled my five siblings and me, but she also has always had younger women around her that she is discipling. I have so many memories of my mom having high school and college-age women over to our home when I was a child. She would teach them the ways of Jesus as she cooked, cleaned, and fed her kids. She would share her own story and journey with Jesus. She would be a listening ear to them as they shared their stories. She was raising up disciples, and many of them became like her, having families of their own and making disciples while raising their children. If you're a mother yourself, see this season as a unique opportunity to disciple both your children and other women to be wholehearted followers of Jesus.

Parents have an incredible opportunity to disciple their children. For parents and grandparents, remember that parenting is an essential part of discipleship and can build a strong foundation in someone's walk with the Lord. Commit to training up your children and grandchildren to be lifelong disciples of Jesus.

DISCIPLESHIP

Steve – Leadership Coach

When I was at Abilene Christian University, I worked with a mission organization there and a mission club called Mission Outreach. I did discipleship with some exchange students from Japan. When I was in St. Louis, Missouri, I served at the county and state jail regularly, conducting Bible studies as I discipled young believers who were in prison. I did mission work in Thailand for sixteen years. During my time there, we did a lot of friendship evangelism, working with Thai students using English as a medium to teach and share our faith. We did a lot of English camps and clubs on university campuses, where much discipleship and evangelism occurred through that. I have a mentor who has walked with me for 28 years, and I have been the recipient of a lot of wisdom and Kingdom teaching through his life. I, in turn, have passed that on to other people. I have been mentoring my spiritual son Zach in Dallas, Texas, for 12 years. I have taught him a lot about fathering and what it looks like to be a godly leader, and how to lead as a man of God. I teach the Kingdom principle that the servant leader is the highest in the Kingdom of God. Those who serve are those who lead in the Kingdom. I do evangelism at the gym consistently, and I recently began discipling a young man I met there for the past three months. I regularly reach out to young leaders to mentor and disciple for four to six weeks, and I pour into them what the Lord has given to me.

DISCIPLESHIP

CHAPTER SEVEN
THE KEY ROLE OF MENTORING

On your journey of discipling others, it is crucial that you seek out someone to disciple and mentor you. Mentorship is a type of discipleship that usually involves an older person investing in a younger person. It is a healthy accountability in your life as you invest in others.

In the journey of life, it is of paramount importance to seek out mentors, those who have more wisdom and life experience than you do. They will help you grow in maturity as you disciple others. I have seen the benefits of having mentors in my own life, and I have been committed to pursuing mentor relationships for several years.

We see this in the example of Timothy and Titus' life. As they discipled others, they had Paul as a mentor in their life, guiding and instructing them. Follow their example; pursue godly mentors who are older and wiser than you, as well as comrades who can run alongside you, and then younger or less mature believers who you can pour into. If you do not have a mentor, ask God to show you who He is highlighting to mentor you.

Once God highlights them be bold in approaching them and ask them if they would be willing to mentor you. Do not wait for someone to offer to mentor you because that rarely happens. Instead, seek them out and ask if they would be willing to mentor you and how you can serve them. The worst that can happen is they say, "No," in which case you can simply ask God to highlight another person to you to ask.

When someone is mentoring you, your role is to listen and learn from them and to bless and serve them. Be proactive in asking them for specific ways that you can do this.

Reflection Questions:

Have you ever had a mentor? If so, what have you learned from them?

If you haven't had a mentor, what would you desire to learn from a mentor?

Who is God highlighting to be a mentor in your life?

Kerrigan – College Student

In my sophomore year of college, I was placed in a group of four other girls who were my age and a mentor who was a couple of years older. Little did I know the amount of beauty that would come from this tender picture of accountability and community. Going through different books and studying in-depth scripture weekly gave me a clearer view of discipleship's importance. The next year, I become an RA (resident assistant) on campus and truly felt a burden to reach out to girls in the dorm that might not step into a campus ministry. This turned into separate weekly meetings with two different girls who are a couple of years younger than me. One girl is new to the faith, and we have been going through the Gospels. The other girl was raised in the church, and we just chose a book from which we take on a chapter a week. Both of these beautiful women challenge me in their hunger to know Christ deeper. Through the relationship between Paul and Timothy in the New Testament, we are reminded of the calling to pour into others and share the promise of the Gospel. Being mentored and mentoring has been a privilege that has amplified my dependence on Jesus.

CHAPTER EIGHT
METHODS FOR DISCIPLESHIP

Now that we've looked at the reasons why discipleship is important, as well as examples of discipleship in scripture and from my own life, we can start looking at exactly how we disciple others. What elements are essential to include when you go about discipling others, and what are some methods we can employ? As Jesus is the ultimate example of discipleship, we will look to Him as our leading example. If you haven't already, I will encourage you to read Chapter 4 of this book before reading this one, where we breakdown the key elements of how Jesus discipled others. This chapter will focus more on practical ways to lead others to engage with God's Word and follow Jesus' example.

The Person of Peace

Looking to Jesus, we see in Luke 10:1-11 that Jesus sends out seventy-two of His followers to go ahead of Him. He sends them out two by two into surrounding towns. He instructs them not to take things with them and to go in a place of trust and dependence on the Lord. This is a picture of dependence in discipleship. We must be in a position of surrender and humility, continually trusting God to lead us and teach us. In this passage, Jesus gives His disciples a valuable indicator of who to look for when they are making disciples. He describes the type of person that they will encounter on their journey of making disciples, a person of peace. This is a person who will welcome them and welcome the Gospel message. As we embark on this discipleship journey, we look for the person of peace who will welcome us and is open to receive the Gospel.

When choosing people to disciple, you want to look for people who are open and welcome to your message and to being discipled. Often, we look for the neediest person we know to disciple. They may be someone who requires help and counsel, but they are not willing to be discipled.

The person(s) you disciple needs to be welcoming to you, and they also need to be open to receive teaching and discipleship based on the Word of God. They need to be willing to listen and obey the commands of Jesus. They need to be a listener and a learner. When you're looking to disciple someone, these characteristics and qualities are key.

Most importantly, you are listening to the guidance of the Holy Spirit to lead and direct you to the right person(s). You want to invest in the person(s) God is leading you to. You don't want to waste your time, energy, and effort on someone who is not receptive. You want to invest in good soil. See the parable of the sower in Matthew 13:1-23. Spend your investment on "good soil" people.

Baptism

Once you find the person highlighted to you to disciple, the first step is to follow the command of Jesus by baptizing them and teaching them to obey everything He has commanded (Matt 28:18-20). The person you are discipling may have already been baptized. If they have, that is great! But if they have not yet been baptized, lead them through the process of salvation and accepting Jesus as the Lord of their life. After they have accepted Jesus, baptize them. If the person you are discipling is not yet a follower of Jesus, you can teach them the Word of God to lead them to a place of surrender to Jesus. The Word of God is power, and it draws people to repentance. You can disciple nonbelievers into salvation, and you can disciple believers into maturity. Whether the person you are discipling is a believer in Jesus or not, you are called to teach them Jesus' commands. Simply put, discipling someone means to teach them the Word of God and lead them by example.

D.B.S. (Discovery Bible Study)

There is no one specific way to disciple. The Holy Spirit will guide you on how to disciple each person that He leads you to. So many tools and methods are available to assist you with your disciple-making journey. I personally like to use one method called the Discovery Bible Study Method—otherwise known as the D.B.S. method.[7] It focuses on scripture, and it uses four simple questions to lead someone through the Bible. You can open to any portion of scripture, read through the passage with the person(s) you are discipling, and ask the following four questions. The first question asks, "What does this passage say about God?" The second question asks, "What does this passage say about people?" The third question is, "How can I obey this passage?" The fourth and final question is, "Who can I share what I learned with?" The D.B.S. model's point is to facilitate discussion, help people discover scripture, and teach them to obey it. This method can be used both in a 1-1 session and in a group context.

Teaching

Another discipleship method can look like reading through a section of scripture, sharing more about it through teaching, and then opening up an

---

[7] Discovery Bible Study

DISCIPLESHIP

opportunity for discussion and questions. Good students ask questions. When you disciple someone, be prepared for questions and know that it is ok not to have all the answers.

When you don't have the answers, practice humility, and simply inform them that you don't know the answer. You could then encourage them to go away and do some self-study to explore the question further (and you could do the same). Be ready to discuss again when you next meet. In discipleship, you don't have to have all the answers. You simply have to be obedient and humble.

As a teacher, you have to be teachable yourself. The beauty of the Bible is that we get to have a personal relationship with the author. Teach the person you are discipling to take their questions directly to the Holy Spirit, who is the great Teacher. He is the one who *"guides us into all truth* (John 16:13)."

Sermon on the Mount

If you are unsure about which biblical passage to start discipling someone with, a great place is the Sermon on the Mount, found in Matthew 5, 6, and 7. In these chapters, we find Jesus' longest recorded sermon. The entire sermon with His teachings. It covers the simple practices of the

Christian faith, such as giving, praying, and fasting, as well as what things to avoid as a Christian. Jesus promises that if you build your life on His teachings, you are *"like a wise man building your house on the rock* (Matt 7:24-27)."

Jesus promises in the Sermon on the Mount that *"whoever does these things and teaches them will be great in the Kingdom of heaven* (Matt 5:19)." We don't strive to be great in the eyes of men, but we seek to be great in the eyes of God! This is a promise of greatness that you can take hold of.

Memorization

Another vital aspect of discipleship is scripture memorization. Part of teaching someone to obey Jesus' commands looks like helping them commit His words to memory.

I recommend giving the person you are discipling regular scripture memory verses to help them grow in their walk with Jesus. When they put scripture to memory, it can help them in their day-to-day life by obeying Jesus and walking as His disciple. Giving them a verse each week to memorize is a helpful practice to assist them in growing in the knowledge of God.

Prayer

Another important aspect of discipleship is prayer. You want to teach your disciple how to pray, just as we see Jesus teach his disciples to pray through the Lord's prayer. Prayer, simply put, is a dialogue with God. You are having a conversation with Him. You are hearing His voice and responding to His leading.

You want to disciple people in the place of prayer. You want them to become a person of prayer. As they grow in maturity in their walk with Jesus, you want hearing His voice to be something they seek and desire. Teach them to be faithful, committed, and attentive in the place of prayer. Teach them how to teach others to pray. Some key passages you can use to teach on prayer is the Lord's prayer in Matthew 6:9-13 and the parable of the persistent widow in Luke 18:1-8. These are passages that speak on the importance of prayer and lay out the foundations of how to do it.

You want the person you disciple to have a thriving relationship with Jesus, and every relationship has to involve communication. Teach the person you are discipling to pray.

My Discipleship Model

Here is an example of how I would typically structure a 1-1 discipleship session. You don't have to follow this model, but it may be a good starting point as you work out what works best for you and those you're discipling.

You want to be in regular contact with those you disciple, either through regular discipleship meetings, informal interactions during your week, or other forms of communication such as text or calls. I start the first ten minutes of the meeting, listening to how the person is doing. Ask questions about their life and how their week has been. With that in mind, it shouldn't take long to get caught up to date with how they are doing at the start of the session as you take an active role and interest in their life.

We then take the next five minutes to review the scripture that they were assigned to memorize the previous week. Then we pray. I pray, or as they grow in confidence, I ask the person I'm discipling to pray and ask the Holy Spirit to reveal Jesus to us through His Word.

We open the Bible to the passage of scripture that we are covering. We spend the next 30 minutes reading through the passage, asking questions, and discussing it. You can use the D.B.S. questions or alternative methods that you've found or developed.

In the last 15 minutes, I ask them for prayer requests and then minister to them by lifting them up in prayer.

DISCIPLESHIP

Reflection Questions:

How is the Lord inviting you to disciple?

What portion of scripture is the Lord highlighting for you to study with the person you are discipling?

Create your own discipleship plan. What passage of scripture will you cover with the person you are discipling? Where will you meet? When will you meet? Will you be meeting in person or over the phone?

DISCIPLESHIP

Neepa - Mom

Discipleship, for me, is the process by which we incorporate the life of Jesus and the lordship of Jesus into our daily lives. Building a relationship with a new believer is a genuine discipleship journey. I met Naina when she was a college student and curious about why I believed in Jesus Christ. Months of discussions about the Lord followed. When Naina committed herself to follow Jesus, our weekly meetings continued with the added depth of a disciplined study of God's Word. We kept in touch during the week and discussed general life issues in the light of the Lord's will as revealed to us. In those times, we talked about future life partners, honoring our parents, service in the community of faith, and a moral lifestyle. Discipleship is life transference. Naina now walks with new believers and shares the Word of God and life with them.

DISCIPLESHIP

CHAPTER NINE
DON'T QUIT!

In discipleship, there will be moments where you feel like giving up. The enemy hates discipleship. He hates you, and he wants to bring discouragement to you. People are imperfect, and they can be challenging. People will fail you, and there will be moments of disappointment and discouragement. There will be times when you feel like giving up. A big part of discipleship involves endurance.

You have to stay the course. You have to be committed to fulfilling the Great Commission even in the midst of discouragement. Amid hardship and difficulty, you must press on. Consistency is key when you disciple someone. Be consistent with them. Do it regularly. Get involved in their life. Care about their journey. Sacrifice for their success. Walk with them through their victories and failures.

You may only have a short window of opportunity to disciple this person. Make the most of the time that you have with them. Have a vision and focus when you enter into discipleship. Communicate that vision to the person you are discipling. Begin the process of discipleship with a clear idea of the outcome. What are the desired results that you want to see at the end of your time discipling them? Who do you want them to become through this process of discipleship? Show them what it's going to take. It will take discipline, and it will take time. You're going to help empower them to walk *"worthy of the calling God has given them* (Col 1:10)."

We see Jesus walking with His twelve disciples for three and a half years. He taught them His ways, and He invited them into a relationship so that they could follow in His footsteps. Even when they deserted him and when they denied Him, Jesus didn't give up on them.

We see the beautiful story of Jesus restoring Peter after he had denied Him in John 21. When Peter felt like a failure, Jesus reminded him of the truth of how He saw him. He called him back to his calling and destiny. After Jesus ascended into heaven, Peter was boldly proclaiming the truth of the Gospel because he had been transformed by walking with Jesus.

Every discipleship journey is different. Sometimes you'll disciple a person for an extended period of time, and sometimes it will be shorter. Some people will be more challenging to disciple, and some will be easy. The Holy Spirit will direct you

DISCIPLESHIP

and show you who to disciple and how long to disciple them.

The goal of discipleship is not that you'll disciple someone for the rest of their life but that you create a legacy by discipling people in a way that they go on to disciple others. The goal is to help move someone along in their spiritual journey, allowing them to grow in spiritual maturity.

In discipleship, you want to pray and ask for the Holy Spirit to show you the duration and amount of time that He wants you to spend with the person(s). Our present lives on this earth are finite, and we can only disciple so many people at a time. You must ask the Holy Spirit who He wants you to disciple right now. Then, when you feel led, ask Him when it's time to end discipleship of a given person or group and when He wants you to start new discipleship journeys with others.

There may be seasons where you are discipling one other person and seasons where you are discipling many. There may be times where you are discipling people in person, and there may be times where you're discipling people long distance. The goal is to always be in a position of discipleship, no matter your season of life, and for the rest of your life.

DISCIPLESHIP

This is your calling as a follower of Jesus. God will highlight to you the people He is calling you to disciple. He will lead, guide, and direct you. You only have to be willing. God is looking for a willing heart.

Reflection Questions:

Think back to your previous discipleship relationships. Were there any that ended up being ineffective or cut short because of inconsistency? Were you the person discipling someone, or were you being discipled? Ask God to reveal His heart on the matter and guide you on how things can be different next time.

Are there any new discipleship relationships you need to pick up this season or any existing ones you need to drop?

Are there any relationships where you need to reconsider your level of time commitment or your approach to discipleship in order to be consistent?

Ask the Lord for wisdom at the beginning of this discipleship process. How is He inviting you to trust Him as you begin this journey with Him?

DISCIPLESHIP

Russ - Missionary to Thailand

As a missionary to Thailand for seventeen years, our team invested our time in many different activities. We taught English to college students to build friendships in order to share the Gospel. We worked with young men who had alcohol and drug addictions. We had outreaches to children in the slums of Thailand. We even went into bars with a ministry that reached out to prostitutes and helped them begin a new life in Christ. However, when I look back at those seventeen years, one thing stands out as bearing the most fruit even until today. We had a Bible study at our house one evening, and as we finished, one of the young women said there was a guy she had met on the bus that had been waiting at the entrance of our neighborhood since the study began. She was hesitant to tell me about him because she perceived that he was attracted to her and was unsure of his motives in coming to the study.

I drove out to find him, and there he was, waiting on the corner in a blue denim jacket. His name was Suwit, and we developed a friendship. I would meet him during his lunch break, and we would study the Bible together and talk about what it meant to follow Jesus. Suwit eventually married the young woman named Ying, who invited him to that Bible study. Through the years, Suwit and Ying became the most faithful disciples in the church. They eventually helped us start a home for abandoned children and helped to pastor the church. My relationship with Suwit was not without conflict. At one point, he didn't talk to me for a whole month because

DISCIPLESHIP

of a misunderstanding that came between us. Today, Suwit continues to pastor and disciple other men in the church he helps lead. His wife Ying has taught young mothers how to train up their children in the ways of the Lord, and they both have raised their children and the kids they have taken in to live their lives for the Gospel. Out of all the things that we chose to invest in, this discipleship relationship bore the most fruit from our seventeen years in Thailand!

DISCIPLESHIP

CHAPTER TEN
JUST START!

It's time to start your process of discipleship! Begin to ask the Lord who He is inviting you to disciple. Look for the person of peace who is welcoming, open, a listener, and a learner.

The enemy hates discipleship, and he hates you. The devil will try to keep you from discipling others. His will use fear and intimidation to try to discourage you, but because we know his schemes, we know how to combat them. The Bible tells us to *"resist the devil, and he will flee from us* (1 Pet 5:9)." We must resist. We must combat fear with faith. We must combat intimidation with the truth. Do not let fear or intimidation keep you from practicing discipleship. Engage in it. Practice it and do it.

Why should we disciple? Because Jesus is worthy of it. Scripture tells us that God desires that *"none should perish but that all would come to repentance* (2 Pet 3:9)." Jesus commanded us to go and proclaim the Gospel and make disciples of all nations. Baptizing them and teaching them to obey his commands (Matt 28:18-20). Jesus desires that we would do this, and He has called us to do it because he is worthy. We must see discipleship as a

DISCIPLESHIP

worthwhile endeavor. It is worth your time, your attention, and your effort. It is his desire for your life that you would engage in discipleship. He wants as many people as possible to be saved, grow in spiritual maturity, and walk in the fullness of their calling. You could be a part of making that happen.

God chooses to use people like us to accomplish His purposes. You are not too young or too old. You are qualified simply because Jesus qualifies you. If you don't feel qualified, that's a great place to be because it means that you're more likely to be dependent on the Holy Spirit to lead and guide you in this endeavor. Do not be afraid and do not be discouraged, for God is with you, and He will empower you!

Go make disciples and change the world!

Reflection Questions:

Are there any specific areas of fear or intimidation that stop you from discipling others?

Are there any verses in scripture that you have previously used to help you overcome your fear in this area?

Ask God to show you some keys to how you can combat areas of fear and intimidation in your discipleship journey. Write them down and ask Him for His grace and peace as you start on a journey of overcoming your fear.

BIBLIOGRAPHY

Understanding the Meaning of the Term "Disciple". (n.d.). Retrieved December 2020, from https://bible.org/seriespage/2-understanding-meaning-term-disciple

Greek word "anthropoi" Bible Gateway 2 Timothy 2:2 Footnote. (n.d.) Retrieved December 2020, from https://www.biblegateway.com/passage/?search=2%20Timothy%202%3A2&version=ESV

5 Steps for Disciple Multiplication. (2018, March 27). Retrieved December 2020, from Christianity Today: https://www.christianitytoday.com/pastors/2018/march-web-exclusives/5-steps-for-disciple-multiplication.html

Adm. McRaven Urges Graduates to Find Courage to Change the World. (2014, May 16). Retrieved December 2020, from https://news.utexas.edu/2014/05/16/mcraven-urges-graduates-to-find-courage-to-change-the-world/

Merriam Webster Dictionary. (n.d.). Retrieved December 2020, from rabbi (noun): https://www.merriam-webster.com/dictionary/rabbi

Who Were Timothy and Titus? (n.d.). Retrieved December 2020, from https://bible.org/seriespage/who-were-timothy-and-titus

Discover Bible Study (n.d). Retrieved December 2020, from A safe place to see for yourself what the Bible says: https://s3.eu-central-1.amazonaws.com/dbsguide/en-US.DBSguide-web.pdf

ABOUT THE AUTHOR

River Lynn is a passionate follower of Jesus, who has a vision to see the church empowered to make disciples. Her life has been transformed by the saving power of Jesus and she desires all to come to the knowledge of Him. River has traveled extensively around the world and has a passion for teaching. River's life ambition is to know Jesus and make Him known.